ANIMALS OF THE ARCTIC

Arctic Foxes

by Rebecca Pettiford

BLASTOFF! READERS 2

BELLWETHER MEDIA • MINNEAPOLIS, MN

Note to Librarians, Teachers, and Parents:

Blastoff! Readers are carefully developed by literacy experts and combine standards-based content with developmentally appropriate text.

Level 1 provides the most support through repetition of high-frequency words, light text, predictable sentence patterns, and strong visual support.

Level 2 offers early readers a bit more challenge through varied simple sentences, increased text load, and less repetition of high-frequency words.

Level 3 advances early-fluent readers toward fluency through increased text and concept load, less reliance on visuals, longer sentences, and more literary language.

Level 4 builds reading stamina by providing more text per page, increased use of punctuation, greater variation in sentence patterns, and increasingly challenging vocabulary.

Level 5 encourages children to move from "learning to read" to "reading to learn" by providing even more text, varied writing styles, and less familiar topics.

Whichever book is right for your reader, Blastoff! Readers are the perfect books to build confidence and encourage a love of reading that will last a lifetime!

This edition first published in 2019 by Bellwether Media, Inc.

No part of this publication may be reproduced in whole or in part without written permission of the publisher. For information regarding permission, write to Bellwether Media, Inc., Attention: Permissions Department, 6012 Blue Circle Drive, Minnetonka, MN 55343.

Library of Congress Cataloging-in-Publication Data

Names: Pettiford, Rebecca, author.
Title: Arctic Foxes / by Rebecca Pettiford.
Description: Minneapolis, MN : Bellwether Media, Inc., 2019. |
  Series: Blastoff! Readers. Animals of the Arctic | Audience: Age 5-8. |
  Audience: K to Grade 3. | Includes bibliographical references and index.
Identifiers: LCCN 2018030952 (print) | LCCN 2018036173 (ebook) |
  ISBN 9781681036595 (ebook) | ISBN 9781626179356 (hardcover : alk. paper)
Subjects: LCSH: Arctic fox--Juvenile literature. | Animals--Arctic regions--Juvenile literature.
Classification: LCC QL737.C22 (ebook) | LCC QL737.C22 P4775 2019 (print) | DDC 599.776/4--dc23
LC record available at https://lccn.loc.gov/2018030952

Editor: Rebecca Sabelko   Designer: Jeffrey Kollock

Printed in the United States of America, North Mankato, MN

Table of Contents

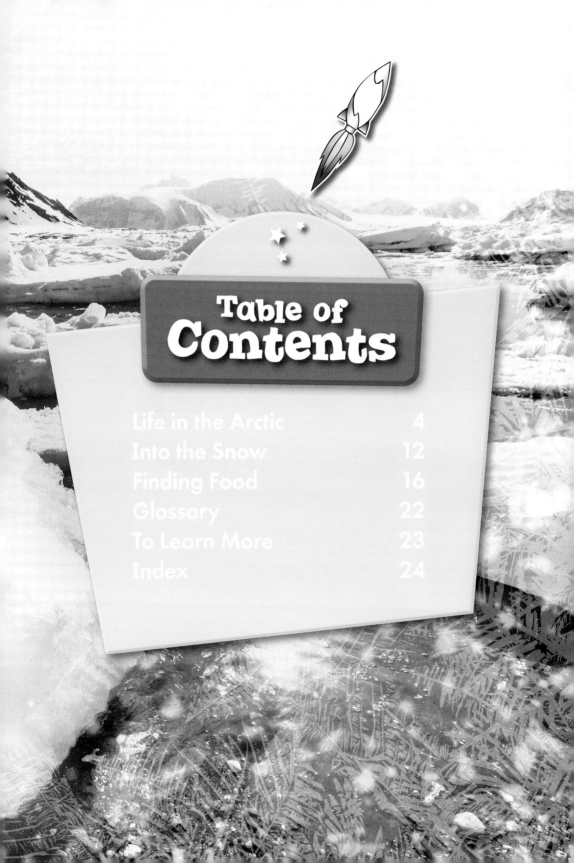

Life in the Arctic

Arctic foxes are built for the Arctic **tundra**.

Thick fur and **bushy** tails keep them warm in this dry and rocky **biome**.

Arctic Fox Range

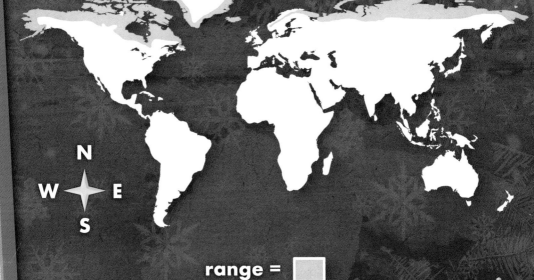

N
W   E
S

range =

Fur on the bottom of their paws keeps Arctic foxes from sliding on ice. It also keeps them warm.

Sharp claws help them
dig for **prey** in the snow.

Their gray summer fur helps Arctic foxes match the color of the rocky land.

summer fur

Special Adaptations

thick, white fur

sharp claws

fur under paws

Their white winter fur makes them hard to see in the snow.

Arctic foxes have short ears that face forward. They also have excellent hearing.

These two **adaptations** help them hear prey move under snow!

Into the Snow

Arctic foxes leap and break through snow to catch prey.

Sometimes, they catch more than they can eat. They hide leftovers in the snow.

Arctic Fox Stats

Least Concern	Near Threatened	Vulnerable	Endangered	Critically Endangered	Extinct in the Wild	Extinct

conservation status: least concern

life span: 3 to 6 years

Arctic foxes dig **dens** in the snow to escape bad weather.

kits

den

Dens are safe places to
stay warm and raise **kits**.

Finding Food

lemming

Arctic foxes are **omnivores**. They like eating small animals like **lemmings** and birds.

They also eat berries,
seaweed, and eggs.

Arctic foxes usually hunt alone.

Arctic Fox Diet

northern collared lemmings

ptarmigans

black crowberries

Sometimes, they form small groups to look for food left by polar bears.

Arctic foxes survive the harsh tundra because of their many adaptations.

This biome is their perfect home!

Glossary

adaptations—changes an animal undergoes over a long period of time to fit where it lives

biome—a large area with certain plants, animals, and weather

bushy—thick and furry

dens—sheltered places

kits—young Arctic foxes

lemmings—small, short-tailed animals with furry feet and small ears

omnivores—animals that eat both plants and animals

prey—animals that are hunted by other animals for food

tundra—rocky land in the Arctic that has a frozen layer of ground and little plant life

To Learn More

AT THE LIBRARY

Jeffries, Joyce. *Arctic Foxes of the Tundra*. New York, N.Y.: KidHaven Publishing, 2017.

Phillips, Dee. *Arctic Fox*. New York, N.Y.: Bearport Publishing, 2015.

Statts, Leo. *Arctic Foxes*. Minneapolis, Minn.: Abdo Zoom, 2017.

ON THE WEB

FACTSURFER

Factsurfer.com gives you a safe, fun way to find more information.

1. Go to www.factsurfer.com.

2. Enter "Arctic foxes" into the search box.

3. Click the "Surf" button and select your book cover to see a list of related web sites.

Index